SPORTING MEMORIES

Cricket

This is a STAR FIRE book

STAR FIRE BOOKS
Crabtree Hall, Crabtree Lane
Fulham, London SW6 6TY
United Kingdom

www.star-fire.co.uk

First published 2008

08 10 12 11 09

1 3 5 7 9 10 8 6 4 2

Star Fire is part of The Foundry Creative Media Company Limited

The CIP record for this book is available from the British Library.

ISBN: 978 1 84786 217 4

Printed in China

Thanks to: Chelsea Edwards, Adnan Zaheer and Nick Wells

Images courtesy of Fotolia: page 19 © Dave Timms; 21 © Jim Giddins; 23 © Sergey Ivanov; 25 ©
edgecreative; 27 © Michael Flippo.

Images courtesy of Mary Evans Picture Library: pages 3, 4, 9, 35, 37, 39, 40, 43, 47, 49, 51, 53, 55,
57, 59, 61, 63, 65, 67, 69, 71, 72.

Images courtesy of Shutterstock: page 7 © Stephen Finn; 11 © afaizal; 13, 15, 17, 29, 31, 45 ©
Lance Bellers; 33 © Laurence Gough.

SPORTING MEMORIES

Cricket

Edited by James Cadogan

STAR FIRE

GREAT GROUNDS
Lord's
Location: London, England

Established:	1787
Capacity:	28,000
End Names:	Pavilion End, Nursery End
Home Team:	Marylebone Cricket Club, Middlesex

GREAT MOMENTS

It was in 1977 that Geoffrey Boycott scored his
hundredth first-class hundred in an Ashes
Test. To make it even more special the
Yorkshireman achieved this feat at a full house
at Headingley. 'If somebody had told me when
I started out I'd score a hundred hundreds I
wouldn't have believed them. But if they'd told
me I'd score my hundredth hundred in front of
a capacity Headingley crowd, against Australia,
I'd have said "you're mad, you're crackers".'

The opening West Indian bowling
partnership of Curtly Ambrose and
Courtney Walsh was legendary. They
worked in tandem for a decade from 1988
onwards, dismissing batsmen with menace,
skill and accuracy. Together they took
421 wickets in 49 Test matches, an
incredible record from two likeable
and capable cricketers.

GREAT CRICKETERS
Sir Viv Richards

Born:	7 March 1952
Place of Birth:	St John's, Antigua
Batting Style:	Right-hand bat
Bowling Style:	Right-arm slow
National Team:	West Indies

GREAT CRICKETERS
Sachin Tendulkar

Born:	24 April 1973
Place of Birth:	Maharashtra, India
Nickname:	Tendlya,
	Little Master
Batting Style:	Right-hand bat
Bowling Style:	Right-arm offbreak,
	Legbreak googly
National Team:	India

GREAT GROUNDS
Eden Gardens

Location: Kolkata, India

Established:	1864
Capacity:	100,000
End Names:	High Court End, Pavilion End
Home Team:	Bengal

GREAT GROUNDS
The Oval

Location: London, England

Established:	1845
Capacity:	23,000
End Names:	Pavilion End, OCS Stand End
Home Team(s):	Surrey, England

GREAT CRICKETERS
Sir Ian Botham

Born:	24 November 1955
Place of Birth:	Cheshire, England
Nickname:	Beefy
Batting Style:	Right-hand bat
Bowling Style:	Right-arm fast-medium

The 2006–07 Ashes series saw Shane
Warne – one of the finest spin bowlers in
history – take his 700th Test wicket.
The final total of Test wickets taken
by Warne during his career stands
at an incredible 708.

GREAT MOMENTS

Ian Botham will always be remembered for
the incredible impact he had on the 1981
Ashes series. Never before has a singular
player turned the game around to such an
extent. With his fantastic batting and
skilled bowling he brought England back
after being 1-0 down in the series to win
the Ashes overall.

GREAT GROUNDS
The Gabba

Location: Queensland, Australia

Established:	1895
Capacity:	42,000
End Names:	Stanley Street End, Vulture Street End
Home Team(s):	Australia, Queensland

GREAT GROUNDS
Melbourne Cricket Ground
Location: Victoria, Australia

Established:	1853
Capacity:	100,000
End Names:	Members End, Great Southern Stand End
Home Team:	The Victorian Bushrangers

GREAT MOMENTS

Don Bradman captured the
imagination of the public on his first
international tour at the tender age
of 21. The Test series was aptly
named 'Bradman versus England'
as he finished the tour with 974
runs including two doubles and
a triple hundred.

GREAT MOMENTS

1947 bore witness to a magnificent English cricket season. The scintillating batting partnership of Denis Compton and Bill Edrich was crucial in England's victory over South Africa and will forever be remembered for setting a record that may never be beaten.

'One-day cricket is an exhibition.
Test cricket is an examination.'

HENRY BLOFELD

There are 10 modes of dismissal in cricket

Caught

Bowled

LBW (Leg before wicket)

Run out

Stumped

Hit wicket

Handled the ball

Double hit

Obstructing the field

Timed out

1936 saw play suspended after Jehangir
Khan's delivery hit a sparrow and wounded
it fatally. The sparrow was stuffed and
mounted on the very ball that killed
it and now lives in the MCC Museum
at Lord's.

GREAT MOMENTS

2005 saw England recapture the Ashes after their last victory in 1986–87. It was an incredible series that was undoubtedly a nail-biter. The Test at Edgbaston was particularly close as England clinched a win by just two runs. The momentous final saw Kevin Pietersen have one of the finest innings in Ashes history that allowed England to draw and therefore win the series overall.

IN AFFECTIONATE REMEMBRANCE
of
ENGLISH CRICKET
Which died at the Oval,
on
29th August, 1882.
Deeply lamented by a large circle
of sorrowing friends and acquaintances.
R.I.P.
N.B.—The body will be cremated, and the
ashes taken to Australia.

'At its best, cricket is the most wonderful
entertainment in the world.'

MICHAEL PARKINSON

Sachin Tendulkar's brilliance as a batsman saw him set a world record for Test-match centuries, as he struck a massive 35 of them during his career in the 1990s.

'Don't bowl him bad balls, he hits the good ones for fours.'

MICHAEL KASPROWICZ

GREAT CRICKETERS
Sir Donald Bradman

Born:	27 August 1908
Died:	25 February 2001
Place of Birth:	New South Wales, Australia
Nickname:	The Don
Batting Style:	Right-hand bat
Bowling Style:	Legbreak
National Team:	Australia

Zimbabwean-born Graeme Hick struck
a record-breaking 405 not out in 1988
against Somerset.

'I can't imagine you will see a greater
innings than Graeme's today'.

IAN BOTHAM

The 1939 Test match between England and South Africa at Durban is the longest Test match on record. This was back when there was no time limitation on Test cricket. The match ended in a draw as the English side had to catch their boat home.

GREAT CRICKETERS
David Gower

Born:	1 April 1957
Place of Birth:	Kent, England
Nickname:	Stoat
Batting Style:	Left-hand bat
Bowling Style:	Right-arm offbreak

Sir Viv Richards is the only person to have played both World Cup cricket and World Cup football. He played for the Antiguan national football team and for the West Indies cricket side.

Bowled indeed

GREAT CRICKETERS
W.G. Grace

Born:	18 July 1848
Died:	23 October 1915
Place of Birth:	Bristol, England
Nickname:	The Doctor
Batting Style:	Right-hand bat

GREAT CRICKETERS
Sir Leonard Hutton

Born:	23 June 1916
Died:	6 September 1990
Place of Birth:	Yorkshire, England
Batting Style:	Right-hand bat
Bowling Style:	Legbreak

GREAT CRICKETERS
Geoffrey Boycott

Born:	21 October 1940
Place of Birth:	Yorkshire, England
Nickname:	Fiery, Boycs
Batting Style:	Right-hand bat
Bowling Style:	Right-arm medium

GREAT MOMENTS

Sir Garfield Sobers smashed his way
into the cricket hall of fame, as in
August 1968 he became the first player
to hit six sixes in an over.

Sir Don Bradman has a staggering batting average of 99.94 and only needed four more runs to ensure an average of 100 at the Oval in 1948. Incredibly and devastatingly he got out on the second ball for a duck.

GREAT CRICKETERS
Brian Lara

Born:	2 May 1969
Place of Birth:	Santa Cruz,
	Trinidad
Batting Style:	Left-hand bat
Bowling Style:	Legbreak googly
National Team:	West Indies

'When you win the toss – bat. If you are in doubt, think about it then bat. If you have very big doubts, consult a colleague – then bat.

W.G. GRACE

GREAT CRICKETERS
Sir Garfield Sobers

Born:	28 July 1936
Place of Birth:	St Michael, Barbados
Batting Style:	Left-hand bat
Bowling Style:	Left-arm fast-medium,
	Slow left-arm orthodox,
	Slow left-arm chinaman
National Team:	West Indies